THE BEST OF
FRANCE
A COOKBOOK

Evie Righter

Recipes by Georgia Downard

CollinsPublishersSanFrancisco

A Division of HarperCollinsPublishers

First published in USA 1992 by Collins Publishers San Francisco

Produced by Smallwood and Stewart Inc.,
New York City

Edited by Melanie Falick

© 1992 Smallwood and Stewart, Inc.

Library of Congress Cataloging-in-Publication Data

Righter, Evie
   The Best of France/Evie Righter.
      p. cm.
   Includes index.
   ISBN 0-00-255086-5
   1. Cookery, French.   I. Title.
   TX719.R53   1992
   641.5944—dc20   91-42838

Printed in Japan by Dai Nippon

Contents

Introduction

One has only to think of France ~ of Brittany and its endless miles of coastline and abundant seafood; of Normandy, where apple trees bloom each spring and cows graze peacefully on lush green fields; and the south, along the Mediterranean, where olive trees bask in the midday sun ~ to understand the richness of the cuisine. Inland, around Lyons, is an area blessed with the best chickens the French can raise and more chefs per household than one can imagine. Then there is the Périgord, land of the truffle and *foie gras*. Consider Burgundy and its rows of heavy, drooping vines; and the wine cellars of Champagne, and the *charcuteries* of Alsace, an area nestled up against the border of Germany. And, lastly, Paris, where chefs and gourmets gather. Combine the magnificent abundance of these areas ~ resources rich beyond belief ~ with a passionate belief in cooking and fine food as a way of life, and then add to those ingredients a talent for preparing food that goes beyond anything called sustenance: What you have is an art form.

A pâtisserie in Provence

The repertoire of preparations in French cuisine is extraordinarily vast and divides into two distinct types: *haute cuisine*, the formal, classically prepared dishes that for years constituted the way of cooking among the restaurants and upper echelons of France and became the model of sophisticated dining the world over; and the everyday ~ the marvelous, soul-satisfying cooking of the home and of *bistros* and *café-restaurants* ~ the comforting flavorful foods, like onion soup, and fricassees and stews that simmer in one pot, like *poulet en cocotte*.

How does one begin categorizing the best recipes of France? It is a little like trying to catalogue the best French paintings from the fifteenth century onward! The task is daunting by virtue of the breadth of choice. But what choices they are! Perhaps the best place to start is with this collection, which is a sampling, really. We have included some of France's most renowned preparations, *soufflés*, for example; bread, there the staff of life; recipes that resonate with some of France's most pronounced flavors, like Provence's *tapenade* and *pissaladière*; dishes of the home, like *pot-au-feu*, boiled dinner, which, depending on where you are in France, might contain meat and chicken, as it does here, or just seafood; and a selection of desserts, one of which capitalizes on the beauty of France's pastry crust, *pâte brisée*, another on the method of caramelizing silken custard.

What you will not find among these pages, for no other reason than constraints of space, are France's more complicated combinations ~ the magnificent *pâtés* and terrines, the *pâte feuilleté*, or puff pastry, and the stunning, multifaceted dishes like *cassoulet*.

To prepare the recipes that follow to the best possible advantage, as the French do, begin with only the freshest ingredients. Take the time to make your own stocks, for example, according to the directions on pages 10-12. And know that in the following recipes, the butter is always unsalted; the eggs are large; the black pepper is freshly ground; the lemon juice is freshly squeezed; and medium-sized pans are used throughout.

As the cuisine of France has evolved over the centuries, it has become more and more refined. And in the last decades we have been witness to movements to reinterpret it. *Nouvelle cuisine* took classic combinations and created imaginative new dishes; *cuisine minceur* was an attempt to reduce or eliminate most of the fat in traditional recipes. Now, at last, we observe a swing back to the basics of French cooking, pure and strong. All that is old is new again, giving proof of the enduring appeal of this timeless cuisine.

Evie Righter

Basic Stocks

Among the building blocks upon which many other French dishes rely are the stocks: chicken, beef, and fish. By using homemade stocks, your soups and sauces will be pure and more flavorful and you will be able to control the amount of sodium they contain.

It is practical and convenient to prepare chicken and beef stocks in advance and freeze them; you might even consider freezing them in ice-cube trays, then transferring the frozen cubes to plastic bags, ready as needed. Fish stock freezes too, but because it can be prepared in a fraction of the time it takes to make the other two ~ 30 or so minutes as opposed to 3 or 4 hours ~ it is often easier to make it fresh.

Fonds de Volaille
Basic Chicken Stock

*3 pounds chicken bones, chopped
into pieces
1 large leek, white part only,
coarsely chopped
1 large carrot, coarsely chopped
1 large celery stalk, coarsely chopped*

*1 onion, studded with 4 cloves
Bouquet garni of 10 parsley stems,
½ teaspoon each dried thyme
& peppercorns, & 1 large bay
leaf (in a cheesecloth bag)*

In a soup kettle, combine all the ingredients with cold water to cover. Bring to a boil, skim the surface, and partially cover.

Simmer, skimming occasionally, for 3 hours. Strain and let cool. **Makes about 6 cups.**

Fonds de Boeuf

Basic Beef Stock

3 pounds beef bones, chopped into
  pieces (use shank, leg, knuckle,
  or neck bones)
1 large onion, quartered
1 large carrot, quartered
1 large celery stalk, quartered
1 small head garlic, unpeeled but
  halved horizontally

1 cup chopped drained tomatoes
Bouquet garni of 12 parsley
  stems, 1 teaspoon dried thyme,
  ½ teaspoon peppercorns, 4 whole
  cloves, & 2 bay leaves (in a
  cheesecloth bag)

Preheat the oven to 450°F. Arrange the bones and vegetables in a large baking pan. Brown in the oven, stirring occasionally, for 25 minutes.

Put the bones and vegetables in a soup kettle, discarding the fat from the baking pan. Add 1 cup water to the baking pan and deglaze it, scraping up the browned bits.

Add the deglazed liquid to the kettle with water to just cover its contents. Add the *bouquet garni,* bring to a boil, skim, and partially cover. Simmer, skimming occasionally, for 3 to 4 hours, or until reduced to about 6 cups. Strain and let cool. **Makes about 6 cups.**

Fumet de Poissons

Basic Fish Stock

1 large onion, sliced

¼ pound mushrooms, sliced

1 tablespoon butter

2 quarts cold water

2 pounds fish bones & trimmings,
    cut into large pieces

1 cup dry white wine

Bouquet garni of 8 parsley stems,
    ½ teaspoon each dried thyme
    & peppercorns, & 1 large
    bay leaf (in a cheesecloth bag)

In a large saucepan over medium heat, cook the onion and mushrooms in the butter, stirring occasionally, for 5 minutes. Add the water and the remaining ingredients. Bring to a boil, skimming, and simmer for 20 minutes. Strain and let cool. **Makes about 6 cups.**

Pâte Brisée

Basic Pastry Dough

France's basic pastry dough ~ *pâte brisée*, literally meaning broken paste ~ differs from its American and English counterparts in that it is a blended dough, intended to be crisp and sturdy, not flaky. To achieve this texture, the dough is kneaded using a technique the French call *fraisage:* actually smearing the dough against the work surface to incorporate the fat. The perfect crust for both sweet and savory fillings alike, *pâte brisée* freezes well, wrapped first in plastic wrap, then in aluminum foil. Store in the freezer for up to three months, then defrost in the refrigerator overnight.

1½ cups all purpose flour

1 stick cold butter, cut into bits

2 tablespoons cold vegetable shortening

¼ teaspoon salt

¼-⅓ cup ice water

In a bowl, combine the flour, butter, shortening, and salt. Blend with fingertips until mixture resembles coarse meal. Add ¼ cup ice water, and toss until incorporated, adding more of the water, if needed, to form a soft dough.

With the heel of your hand, press batches of the dough away from you on a floured surface, smearing it about 6 inches in order to blend and smooth it completely. Form the dough into a ball, wrap it in plastic wrap, and chill for 30 minutes. **Makes enough dough for one 10-inch tart.**

Tapenade

Anchovy and Olive Spread

Anchovies, olives, capers, fresh herbs, and garlic ~ these are
the beloved, bold ingredients of the cuisine of southern
France, and Provence in particular. Use *tapenade* as a spread,
as a dip, or even as a filling for hard-boiled eggs.

*1 (2-ounce) can flat anchovy fillets,
    drained & patted dry*
*1 cup black olives, preferably oil-
    cured or Kalamata, pitted*
2 tablespoons drained capers
*1 teaspoon minced fresh thyme or
    ¼ teaspoon dried, crumbled*

*1 teaspoon minced fresh rosemary or
    ¼ teaspoon dried, crumbled*
1 large garlic clove, chopped
*2 to 3 teaspoons fresh lemon juice,
    or to taste*
¼ cup extra-virgin olive oil
Freshly ground black pepper

In a food processor, combine the anchovies, olives, capers, thyme, rosemary, garlic, and lemon juice, and process until smooth. With the motor running, add the oil in a stream. Transfer the *tapenade* to a small bowl and season with the pepper. Serve at room temperature with toasted bread rounds, called *croûtes* in France. **Makes about 1 cup.**

An outdoor café, Arles

Pissaladière

Niçoise Onion Tart

This is French pizza ~ from Provence, and specifically Nice, and it is superb as a snack or light luncheon dish. It gets its name from a seasoning called *pissalat* (a mixture of anchovy purée, olive oil, cloves, thyme, bay leaf, and pepper) that is traditionally used to coat the uncooked *pissaladière*. Because *pissalat* is very difficult to find away from the Mediterranean, many versions have been developed without it.

2 recipes Pâte Brisée (p. 13)

5 tablespoons extra-virgin olive oil

1 pound onions, thinly sliced

½ teaspoon each dried thyme, basil, & rosemary, all crumbled

Salt & pepper

1 (16-ounce) can tomatoes, drained & chopped

3 large garlic cloves, minced

2 tablespoons dried bread crumbs

¼ cup freshly grated Parmesan

2 to 3 (½ pound) firm ripe plum tomatoes, cored, seeded, & thinly sliced

1 (2-ounce) can flat anchovy fillets, drained (optional)

Pitted black niçoise olives

Minced fresh basil, chives, or parsley for garnish

On a floured surface, roll the dough into a round ¼ inch thick and transfer it to a heavy baking sheet. Crimp the edge decoratively and prick the bottom with a fork. Chill for 30 minutes.

In a large skillet over medium heat, add 3 tablespoons of the oil and cook the onions, herbs, and salt and pepper, stirring occasionally, until golden. Add the canned tomatoes and garlic, and cook, stirring,

until the liquid is evaporated. Set aside.

Preheat the oven to 450°F. Sprinkle the crust with the bread crumbs and smooth the onion filling over it. Sprinkle with half the Parmesan, top with the fresh tomatoes, and brush with the remaining 2 tablespoons of oil. Decorate the top with the anchovies and olives. Bake for 30 to 35 minutes, or until the pastry is golden brown.

Before serving, sprinkle the tart with the remaining Parmesan and the fresh herbs. Let cool for 10 minutes before slicing. Serve warm or at room temperature. **Serves 16 as an hors d'oeuvre.**

Mousse de Saumon Fumé

Smoked Salmon Mousse

When you see the word *mousse* as it applies to French cooking, think foam ~ a delicate, airy mixture that begins as a purée, and is then lightened with a variety of ingredients, the two most frequent being cream or egg whites. This savory *mousse* can be enjoyed, thanks to the food processor, in what amounts to the mere flick of a switch.

8 ounces cream cheese, cut into
    pieces & softened
6 ounces smoked salmon, cut into
    1-inch pieces
3 tablespoons sour cream
Lemon juice, to taste

Salt
½ cup heavy cream, whipped
Salmon caviar for garnish
Toasted herbed croûtes or assorted
    crackers as accompaniments

In a food processor, blend the cream cheese, salmon, sour cream, lemon juice, and salt until smooth. Transfer the mixture to a bowl and fold in the whipped cream gently but completely. Chill, covered, for at least 2 hours. Garnish with the caviar and serve with *croûtes* or crackers. **Makes about 2 cups.**

Soupe à l'Oignon Gratinée

Onion Soup au Gratin

Onion soup is the best of basic French cooking, warming the soul as well as the body. Use a flavorful homemade stock, if possible. The large toasts are optional but recommended.

1½ pounds onions, thinly sliced

3 tablespoons butter

Salt & pepper

⅛ teaspoon sugar

2 tablespoons flour

6 cups homemade Beef Stock (p. 11)
    or canned broth

½ cup dry white wine

Bouquet garni of 8 parsley stems,
    ½ teaspoon dried thyme,
    6 peppercorns, & 1 bay leaf
    (in a cheesecloth bag)

2 tablespoons cognac

8 slices of French bread, cut
    1 inch thick

2 tablespoons butter, melted

1 garlic clove, halved

1 cup grated Gruyère cheese

⅓ cup freshly grated Parmesan

In a large covered saucepan over medium-low heat, cook the onions in the butter with the salt and pepper, stirring occasionally, until soft. Add the sugar and cook over medium heat, uncovered, stirring occasionally, until the onions are golden brown. Add the flour and cook, stirring, for 3 minutes. Add the stock, wine, *bouquet garni,* and salt and pepper, and cook, partially covered, skimming occasionally,

for 30 minutes. Stir in the cognac.

Preheat the oven to 350°F and the broiler. Arrange the bread on a baking sheet, brush both sides with some of the melted butter, and bake, turning once, for 15 minutes, or until golden. Rub the slices with the garlic.

Remove the *bouquet garni* and pour the soup into four ovenproof bowls. Completely cover the top of each bowl with the toasts. Sprinkle the toasts with the cheeses and drizzle with the remaining melted butter. Bake the soup for 15 to 20 minutes, or until simmering. Run under the broiler until the cheese is golden. **Serves 4.**

Crème de Cresson

CREAM OF WATERCRESS SOUP

French soups are justly renowned, with the repertoire ranging from the clearest *consommés* to the heartiest *potages*. The vast majority begin with a chicken, beef, or fish stock and feature vegetables. Some, like the one that follows, are enriched with cream at the end.

3 tablespoons butter

1 large bunch watercress leaves, rinsed & patted dry

1 red potato, peeled & thinly sliced

Salt & pepper

3 tablespoons flour

3 cups Chicken Stock (p.10) or canned broth

½ cup heavy cream

Watercress leaves for garnish

In a saucepan over medium-low heat, melt the butter. Add the watercress, potato, and salt and pepper, and cook, covered with a buttered round of wax paper and the lid, for 15 minutes, stirring occasionally. Add the flour and cook, stirring, for 3 minutes. Add the stock, bring to a boil, and simmer, stirring occasionally, for 15 minutes.

In a food processor, purée the soup in batches and return it to the pan. Add the cream and salt and pepper, and cook over medium-low heat, stirring, until heated through. Serve in bowls and garnish with the remaining watercress leaves. **Serves 4.**

Soupe de Poireaux et Pommes de Terre

Leek and Potato Soup

French cooks, who long ago discovered how well leek and potato work together, have successfully paired these two root vegetables in a variety of dishes, including soups, gratins, and even stews. When preparing this soup, it is important to take the time to clean the leeks thoroughly as a considerable amount of sand lurks within the tightly closed leaves.

1½ pounds boiling potatoes, peeled
& cut into 1-inch pieces
1½ pounds leeks, white part only,
washed, drained, & chopped
½ cup minced celery

6 cups Chicken Stock
(p.10) or canned broth
Salt & pepper
1 cup heavy cream
Minced fresh chives for garnish

In a large saucepan, combine the potatoes, leeks, celery, stock, and salt and pepper. Bring the mixture to a boil and simmer, covered, for 40 minutes, or until the vegetables are tender.

In a food processor or blender, purée the soup in batches and return it to the saucepan. Add the cream and salt and pepper, and bring the soup just to a simmer. Cook over low heat for 5 minutes. Serve hot or cold. Before serving, garnish with the chives. **Serves 4.**

North of Valence, Vercours

Pipérade

Open-Faced Omelet with Onions, Peppers, and Tomatoes

The flavorful Basque sauce that tops this open-faced omelet can also accompany chicken cutlets or cheese dishes, custards, or even a soufflé.

*¼ pound smoked ham, cut into
        julienne strips*
2 tablespoons butter
2 tablespoons olive oil
1 onion, thinly sliced
*1 small green bell pepper, seeded &
        thinly sliced*

Salt & pepper
2 garlic cloves, minced
*1 (16-ounce) can whole peeled
        tomatoes, drained & chopped*
6 eggs
2 teaspoons water
2 tablespoons minced fresh parsley

In a skillet over medium heat, cook the ham in half the butter and oil, stirring occasionally, for 5 minutes, or until lightly browned. With a slotted spoon, transfer the ham to a plate.

Add the onion, bell pepper, and salt and pepper to the skillet, and cook, stirring occasionally, for 3 minutes. Add the garlic and tomatoes and cook, stirring occasionally, for 4 minutes more, or until dry. Stir

in the ham and cover to keep warm.

In a bowl, whisk together the eggs, water, and salt and pepper. In a large non-stick skillet, heat the remaining butter and oil over medium-high heat until hot. Add the egg mixture to the skillet, stir several times, then stop stirring and cook until just set. Spoon the vegetables and ham over the top. Sprinkle with the parsley and serve immediately. **Serves 4 to 6.**

Quiche au Fromage de Gruyère

Swiss Cheese Quiche

The popularity of quiche knows no bounds. The French tart
can be served in small pieces as an hors d'oeuvre or in
heartier slices as a luncheon entrée. Toss together a green
salad as an accompaniment. A quiche will puff up while
baking; should you reheat it, know that it will not rise again.

1 recipe Pâte Brisée (p. 13)

3 eggs

1½ cups milk

½ cup heavy cream

2 to 3 teaspoons Dijon mustard

Freshly grated nutmeg

Salt & pepper

1 cup grated Gruyère cheese

1 tablespoon butter, cut into bits

On a floured surface, roll the dough into a ⅛-inch-thick round and fit it into a 9-inch tart pan. Chill for 30 minutes.

Preheat the oven to 400°F. Line the pastry shell with a round of wax paper, weight it with uncooked rice or dried beans, and place it on a baking sheet in the middle of the oven. Bake the pastry shell for 10 minutes, or until set. Remove the rice or beans and wax paper, and bake the pastry for 5 minutes more. Let cool slightly. Lower the oven temperature to 375°F.

In a bowl, thoroughly whisk together the eggs, milk, heavy cream, mustard, nutmeg, and salt and pepper. Stir in the cheese. Set the shell on the baking sheet, pour in the filling, and dot with the butter. Bake in the upper third of the oven for 25 to 30 minutes, or until puffed and golden. **Serves 6.**

Soufflé au Fromage

Cheese Soufflé

The key to making any *soufflé* lies in the way the aerated egg whites are folded into the flour-based sauce; this should be done very gently so that you do not deflate the air you have just beaten in. In fact, it is even acceptable to leave some of the egg white unincorporated.

3 tablespoons butter

2 tablespoons flour

1 cup milk

2 teaspoons Dijon mustard

Freshly grated nutmeg

Salt & pepper

4 egg yolks

⅔ cup freshly grated Gruyère cheese

⅓ cup freshly grated Parmesan

5 egg whites

Preheat the oven to 425°F. Butter a 4-cup *soufflé* dish and fit it with a buttered wax paper collar extending 3 inches above the rim.

In a saucepan over medium-low heat, melt the butter, add the flour, and cook, whisking, for 3 minutes. Add the milk, mustard, nutmeg, and salt and pepper, and simmer, whisking occasionally, for 5 minutes. Remove the pan from the heat and whisk in the yolks, one at a time. Stir in the Gruyère and ¼ cup of the Parmesan.

In the large bowl of an electric mixer, beat the egg whites until they hold stiff peaks. Stir one quarter of them into the yolk mixture. Gently fold in the remaining whites. Pour into the *soufflé* dish and sprinkle with the remaining Parmesan. Place the *soufflé* dish in the lower third of the oven and reduce the oven temperature to 375°F. Bake for 25 to 30 minutes, or until puffed and browned. Remove the collar and serve at once. **Serves 4 to 6.**

Moules Poulette

Mussels in Egg and Cream Sauce

Not long ago, there were countries in the world where mussels were considered inedible. Fortunately for us all, French cooks never had that bias, understanding as they did just how full and fragrant these mollusks are. In Brittany and Normandy, in particular, but throughout France, mussels are served in soups, salads, and stews. The most simple rendition ~ *moules marinière* ~ steams them with just a touch of onion and wine. In this variation, egg and cream are added to enrich the salty, striking flavor of the strained cooking liquid.

½ cup minced shallots

2 tablespoons butter

4 pounds mussels, scrubbed &

debearded

1 cup dry white wine

½ cup heavy cream

2 large egg yolks

¼ cup minced parsley

Lemon juice, to taste

Salt & pepper

In a large saucepan over medium heat, cook the shallots in the butter, stirring occasionally, for 3 minutes. Add the mussels and wine and cover the pan. Steam the mussels, shaking the pan occasionally, for 5 to 7 minutes, or until the shells have opened. Discard any unopened shells.

With a slotted spoon, transfer the mussels to a serving dish and keep them warm.

Strain the broth through a sieve lined with a double thickness of cheesecloth into a medium saucepan. Over medium-high heat, reduce the strained cooking liquid to 1 cup. In a bowl, whisk together the heavy

cream and egg yolks. Reduce the heat under the saucepan to low, add the cream mixture, and whisk, until thickened slightly. Add the parsley, lemon juice, and salt and pepper, and pour the sauce over the mussels. Toss the mussels with the sauce and serve immediately in soup bowls. **Serves 4.**

Soupe de Poissons

Seafood Soup

The fish soups of France are as varied in content and flavor as the pastel-colored seaside towns and bustling ports where they are made. The one that follows features red snapper, shrimp, mussels, and clams. Serve with a fresh *baguette* and a light red wine and imagine that you are dining on a *quai* in Marseilles.

2½ cups chopped white part of leeks

1 cup chopped fennel bulb

4 garlic cloves, chopped

¼ cup olive oil

1 cup dry white wine

6 cups Fish Stock (p. 12)
    or canned broth

2 cups water

3 cups peeled, seeded, & chopped
    tomatoes, or 3 cups drained
    & chopped canned tomatoes

2 tablespoons tomato paste

1 teaspoon dried basil

1 teaspoon dried savory

½ teaspoon fennel seeds, crushed

1 bay leaf

Salt & pepper

6 hard-shelled clams, washed

6 mussels, scrubbed & debearded

1 pound red snapper fillet or similar
    white fish, cut into 2-inch
    pieces

1 pound large shrimp, shelled
    & deveined

In a large casserole over medium heat, cook the leek, fennel, and garlic in the olive oil, stirring occasionally, for 5 min-utes. Add the wine, fish stock, water, tomatoes, tomato paste, basil, savory, fen-nel seeds, bay leaf, and salt and pepper,

and bring the liquid to a boil. Simmer the mixture, stirring and skimming occasionally, for 30 minutes.

In a food processor, purée the soup in batches and return it to the casserole. Bring the soup to a simmer and add the clams and mussels. Cover the casserole and cook the shellfish over medium-high heat for 5 to 7 minutes, or until the shells have opened. With a slotted spoon, transfer the shellfish to a bowl and cover loosely to keep warm.

Add the red snapper and shrimp to the casserole and simmer, stirring occasionally, for 5 minutes, or until the fish and shrimp are firm to the touch.

Divide the clams and mussels among six bowls and ladle the fish, shrimp, and soup over them. Serve with crusty French bread. **Serves 6.**

Poisson en Papillote

Fish in Parchment

The French method of cooking *en papillote*, or in a paper bag, is wonderful for preserving natural flavors and retaining moisture. It is also quite healthful: The only cooking fat in this recipe is butter, and that is only a minimal amount for greasing the "bag." Food prepared *en papillote* also makes for a dramatic presentation. Just be careful to direct the steam away from yourself and other diners when opening the bags.

1½ pounds striped bass or similar fish fillets

2 carrots, trimmed, peeled, & cut into julienne strips

1 red bell pepper, cored, seeded, & cut into julienne strips

¼ pound snow peas, trimmed

½ cup minced scallions

Salt & pepper

Cut the fish fillets crosswise into four equal pieces.

In a saucepan of boiling salted water, blanch the carrots and bell pepper for 2 minutes. Add the snow peas, bring the water back to a boil, and immediately drain the vegetables. Refresh the vegetables under cold running water and pat dry.

Preheat the oven to 425°F. Using parchment paper, cut out four heart shapes, each measuring about 12 inches long through the center. Butter one side of each

heart, then place a piece of the fillet in the center of each buttered side. Surround each piece of fish with some of the vegetables and sprinkle with the scallions and salt and pepper. Fold the unbuttered side of the heart over each fish. Beginning with the top rounded edge of each heart, fold and crimp the sides of the hearts together to seal the packets. Arrange the packets on a baking sheet and bake for 15 minutes.

Transfer the packets to serving plates and with scissors cut a cross in the top of each one. Fold back the edges and serve immediately. **Serves 4**.

Poulet Sauté Grand-Mère

Sautéed Chicken with Bacon and Potatoes

This recipe demonstrates how chicken was and is still cooked in the French home, traditionally, by grandmothers ~ hence the name, *grand-mère*. This is home-style cooking at its finest. Serve with a green vegetable.

1 (3½-pound) chicken, cut into 8
    pieces, rinsed, & patted dry

Flour for dredging

Salt & pepper

3 tablespoons butter

1 tablespoon vegetable oil

¾ pound small white onions, peeled

½ pound mushrooms, quartered

½ cup dry white wine

2 cups Chicken Stock (p. 10)
    or canned broth

1 tablespoon tomato paste

1 teaspoon dried tarragon

1 teaspoon dried thyme

¼ pound slab bacon, diced, blanched
    in boiling water for 5 minutes,
    & drained

½ pound potatoes, peeled & cut into
    ½-inch pieces

Dredge the chicken in the flour and season with salt and pepper. In a large deep skillet over medium-high heat, warm 2 tablespoons of the butter and the oil until hot. Add the chicken and brown it on all sides. Transfer to a plate. Add the onions and the mushrooms to the skillet, season with salt and pepper, and sauté, stirring, until the onions are golden. Add the wine and cook to reduce the liquid by half. Stir in the stock, tomato paste, tarragon, and thyme. Return the chicken to the skillet and bring

Fields in mist, Périgord

the liquid to a boil. Cover and simmer for 30 to 35 minutes, or until the juices run clear when the chicken is pierced with a fork.

While the chicken cooks, in a separate skillet over medium heat, melt the remaining 1 tablespoon butter. Add the bacon and cook, stirring occasionally, until lightly browned but not crisp. Using a slotted spoon, transfer the bacon to paper towels to drain. Add the potatoes to the skillet and cook over medium-high heat, turning them often, for 5 to 7 minutes, or until golden brown and tender.

Using a slotted spoon, arrange the potatoes and chicken mixture on a platter and top with the bacon. Over medium heat, reduce the cooking liquid in the skillet until thickened, then pour it over the chicken and potatoes. **Serves 4 to 6.**

Poulet aux Quarante Gousses d'Ail

Chicken with Forty Cloves of Garlic

The very idea of cooking forty cloves of garlic would be
unthinkable were it not for the fact that the garlic cooks gently,
poaches actually, turning soft in texture and sweet in flavor.
Don't even think of throwing the garlic away once the chicken is
cooked: Spread it on fresh bread as you would butter.

6 tablespoons butter, softened

1 tablespoon vegetable oil

1 (3½-pound) chicken, cut into
    8 pieces, rinsed, & patted dry

Salt & pepper

2 heads garlic, unpeeled & blanched
    in boiling water for 10 minutes

½ teaspoon dried thyme

1 bay leaf

½ cup dry white wine

1 cup Chicken Stock (p. 10)
    or canned broth

In a large, deep skillet over medium-high heat, warm 2 tablespoons of the butter and the oil until hot. Add the chicken, season with salt and pepper, and brown it on all sides. Distribute the garlic cloves around the chicken and season with the thyme and bay leaf. Cover the skillet and cook the chicken over medium-low heat for 30 to 35 minutes, or until the juices run clear when the chicken is pierced with a fork. Transfer the chicken and garlic to a platter and keep warm. Discard the bay leaf. Skim and discard the fat from the pan, add the wine, and reduce the liquid by half over high heat. Add the stock and reduce to ¾ cup. Remove the pan from the heat and swirl in the remaining 4 tablespoons butter. Pour the sauce over the chicken. **Serves 4 to 6.**

Poulet en Cocotte

Braised Chicken with Vegetables

Cooking braised chicken in a casserole, or *en cocotte*, retains the bird's marvelous moisture and flavor. Accompany this classic casserole with *cornichons*, French gherkins.

1 (3½-pound) chicken, rinsed &
   patted dry
1 teaspoon dried thyme, crumbled
1 teaspoon dried rosemary, crumbled
Salt & pepper
3 tablespoons vegetable oil
¼ pound slab bacon, diced,
   blanched in boiling water for
   5 minutes, & drained
1 large onion, coarsely chopped
2 carrots, coarsely chopped
2 celery stalks, coarsely chopped

2 garlic cloves, minced
½ pound mushrooms, sliced
1 cup dry white wine
1 cup drained & chopped tomatoes
1½ cups Chicken Stock (p. 10)
   or canned broth
Beurre manié made by kneading
   together 2 tablespoons butter
   with 2 tablespoons flour
Minced fresh chives and parsley
   for garnish

Preheat the oven to 400°F. Sprinkle the inside of the chicken with half the thyme and rosemary and season it with salt and pepper. Truss the chicken.

In a casserole over medium-high heat, warm the oil until hot. Add the chicken, brown it on all sides, and transfer it to a plate. Add the bacon to the casserole and cook it over medium heat, stirring, until crisp. With a slotted spoon, transfer the

bacon to paper towels to drain.

Add the onion, carrots, celery, and garlic to the casserole and cook over medium-low heat, covered, stirring occasionally, for 5 minutes. Add the mushrooms and cook over medium heat, stirring occasionally, for 5 minutes more. Add the wine and reduce it by half. Add the browned chicken, tomatoes, stock, the remaining thyme and rosemary, and salt and pepper, and bring the liquid to a boil. Cover the casserole, place it in the oven, and braise the chicken for 50 minutes to 1 hour, or until the juices run clear when the thigh is pricked with a fork.

Transfer the chicken to a serving platter. Skim the fat from the surface of the cooking liquid. Place the casserole on the stovetop and, over high heat, reduce the cooking liquid to 1½ cups. Whisk in the *beurre manié*, a little at a time, until the sauce thickens slightly. Carve the chicken and spoon the sauce and vegetables over it. Sprinkle with the bacon and garnish with the chives and parsley. **Serves 4 to 6.**

Steak au Poivre

Sirloin Steak with Crushed Peppercorns

For meat-lovers, the pleasures of a well-seasoned steak are unforgettable, and what follows is an example of one of the best-seasoned steaks of all. Coarsely crushed peppercorns are pressed into both sides of the meat; it is then sauced with a reduction of the pan juices. The dish is sometimes flambéed in restaurants, but this is really no more than an act of showmanship, and you needn't go to that length. Do accompany it with *pommes frites* and a garnish of fresh watercress, as is the French tradition.

2 teaspoons black peppercorns, crushed

2 teaspoons white peppercorns, crushed

1 (2-pound) boneless sirloin steak, 1½ inches thick

Salt

2 tablespoons vegetable oil

2 tablespoons butter

⅓ cup minced shallots

1 tablespoon flour

¼ cup cognac or brandy

1 cup Beef Stock (p. 11) or canned broth

2 tablespoons minced fresh parsley

Press the peppercorns into both sides of the steak and let stand for at least 30 minutes. Season with salt.

In a large skillet over medium-high heat, warm the oil until hot. Add the steak and cook for 4 minutes on each side for rare. With tongs, transfer to a platter and keep warm.

Discard the fat from the skillet. Add 1 tablespoon butter and the shallots, and cook over medium heat, stirring, for 2 minutes. Add the flour and cook, stirring, for 1 minute. Add the cognac and reduce, stirring, for 1 minute. Add the stock, bring to a boil, and simmer, stirring occasionally, for 3 minutes. Swirl in the remaining butter and the parsley, and pour the sauce over the steak. **Serves 4 to 6.**

Entrecôte Bordelaise

Steak in Red Wine and Shallot Sauce with Beef Marrow

This entrée demonstrates the simple but masterful
French method of sauce-making. You begin with a beef stock
as a foundation ~ and the more flavorful it is the
better ~ which you reduce and season accordingly. Marrow,
the filling of the leg bone, is added as a
garnish and elevates this dish into the category of *haute
cuisine*. Buy marrow at the butcher and, before
adding it to the sauce, poach it in simmering water, ideally
in one piece, for two or three minutes.

1 cup red Bordeaux wine

⅓ cup minced shallots

2 cups Beef Stock (p. 11) or
    canned broth

Beurre manié made by kneading
    together 2 tablespoons butter
    with 2 tablespoons flour

4 to 6 ounces poached beef marrow,
    or to taste (optional)

4 steaks such as shell, club, or
    sirloin, 1 inch thick

Salt & pepper

1 tablespoon olive oil

1 tablespoon butter

In a small heavy saucepan over medium-high heat, combine the wine and shallots and reduce the mixture to ½ cup. Add the stock and reduce the mixture by half. Reduce the liquid to a simmer and add the *beurre manié* a little at a time, whisking, until the sauce is thickened. Add the marrow (if using) to the sauce. Cover the sauce with a buttered round of wax paper to keep warm.

Pat the steaks dry with paper towels, then season them with salt and pepper. In a large skillet over medium-high heat, warm the oil and butter until hot. Add the steaks, without crowding them, and sauté for 3 to 4 minutes per side for medium-rare. Transfer to a platter and cover to keep warm.

With a slotted spoon, remove the marrow from the sauce and slice it. Divide the sauce among four serving plates. Place a steak over each serving of sauce and garnish the meat with slices of marrow. **Serves 4.**

Pot-au-Feu

Boiled Beef with Chicken and Assorted Vegetables

This boiled dinner is basic peasant cooking at its best and can
be prepared with still more ingredients to intensify the
fundamental flavors. Some French cooks add oxtails, or at
least another cut of beef with bones, to strengthen the broth.
Others add cabbage or potatoes. Traditional accompaniments
include coarse salt, pickles, horseradish, and mustard. A sauce
such as an herb mayonnaise can be served, too.

1 (3-pound) rump roast, tied

2 pounds veal bones, chopped into
    2-inch pieces

2 large onions, each stuck with 2
    whole cloves

2 carrots, sliced

1 large celery stalk with leaves, sliced

6 garlic cloves, halved

Bouquet garni of 12 parsley stems,
    8 peppercorns, 1 bay leaf, &
    1½ teaspoons dried thyme
    (in a cheesecloth bag)

6 cups homemade Beef Stock (p. 11)
    or canned broth

Salt

1 (4-pound) stewing chicken,
    cleaned & trussed

6 whole carrots, quartered lengthwise
    & tied together with string

6 medium leeks, white part only,
    halved crosswise & lengthwise,
    rinsed, & tied together with
    string

6 celery stalks, halved crosswise &
    lengthwise, rinsed, & tied
    together with string

6 turnips, peeled & quartered

1 pound smoked garlic sausage,
    such as kielbasa

Fresh thyme leaves for garnish

In a soup kettle, combine the rump roast, veal bones, onions, sliced carrots, sliced celery, garlic, *bouquet garni*, stock, salt, and water to cover. Bring the liquid to a boil and simmer, partially covered, skimming frequently, for 1½ hours. Add the chicken to the pot, return the liquid to a boil, and simmer the mixture, partially covered, skimming occasionally, for 1½ hours.

With a large fork, transfer the meat and chicken to a platter, skim the fat from the surface of the cooking liquid, and strain the liquid through a sieve into a large bowl. Return the meat and chicken to the kettle and add the strained cooking liquid. Bring the liquid to a boil and add the bundles of vegetables (carrots, leeks, and celery). Simmer the vegetables, partially covered, for 10 minutes. Add the turnips and the sausage and simmer, partially covered, for 20 to 30 minutes, or until the vegetables and meat are tender.

Serve in one course directly from the pot or as two courses: first the broth, then a platter of the meat and vegetables. Garnish with the fresh thyme. **Serves 8 to 10.**

Choucroute Garnie

Sauerkraut with Sausage and Smoked Pork

From the province of Alsace, located between the Vosges Mountains and the Rhine River and right on the border of Germany, comes this classic preparation of sauerkraut and sausages. Serve with boiled potatoes and mugs of Alsatian beer or wine glasses full of a good Riesling.

¼ pound slab bacon, diced, blanched in boiling water for 5 minutes, & drained

1 tablespoon butter

1 large onion, thinly sliced

1 carrot, thinly sliced

2 pounds sauerkraut, rinsed & drained well

1½ cups Beef Stock (p. 11) or canned broth

1 cup dry white wine

Bouquet garni of 12 parsley stems, 6 black peppercorns, 6 juniper berries, & 1 bay leaf, (in a cheesecloth bag)

Salt & pepper

2 tablespoons vegetable oil

2 smoked bratwursts, pricked

2 unsmoked veal sausages, pricked

4 slices smoked pork tenderloin, 1 inch thick, or 4 smoked pork chops

½ pound smoked garlic sausage, such as kielbasa, pricked & halved

In a casserole over medium heat, cook the bacon in the butter, stirring, for 3 minutes. Add the onion and carrot and cook, stirring, for 5 minutes. Add the sauerkraut and cook, stirring occasionally, for 5 minutes longer. Add the beef stock, wine, *bouquet garni,* and salt and pepper, and simmer the mixture, covered, for 30 minutes.

In a large skillet over medium heat, warm the oil until hot. Add the bratwursts and veal sausages and cook until the sausages are browned. Transfer to the casserole. Add the sliced pork and garlic sausage to the skillet and cook until browned on both sides. Transfer them to the casserole and stir gently to cover all the meats with the sauerkraut. Simmer the mixture, covered, for 20 to 30 minutes, or until the meat is tender and cooked through. **Serves 4 to 6.**

Côtes de Veau aux Herbes avec Sauce Madère

Herbed Veal Chops in Madeira Sauce

Sauce Madère is of the timeless repertory of French sauces that begin with beef stock, and it is especially recommended to accompany veal, as well as beef and ham. Canned beef broth may be used, but to reap the maximum rewards from this subtle combination, homemade stock is preferred as a base. Serve with the Braised Belgian Endive on page 60.

4 rib veal chops, 1 inch thick

Flour for dredging

Salt & pepper

3 tablespoons vegetable oil

1 tablespoon minced fresh tarragon
   or 1 teaspoon dried

2 teaspoons minced fresh thyme or
   ½ teaspoon dried

⅓ cup minced shallots

½ cup dry white wine

2 cups Beef Stock (p. 11)
   or canned broth

1 tablespoon arrowroot dissolved
   in 2 to 3 tablespoons dry
   Madeira, or to taste

1 to 2 tablespoons softened butter,
   cut into bits, or to taste

2 tablespoons minced fresh chives

Preheat the oven to 400°F. Dredge the veal chops in the flour, shaking off the excess, then season them with salt and pepper. In a large ovenproof skillet over medium-high heat, warm the oil until hot. Add the chops and cook for 3 to 4 minutes on each side, or until golden brown. Sprinkle them with the tarragon and thyme. Bake the chops for 10 minutes, or until firm but still slightly springy to the touch. Using a

fork, transfer the chops to a platter and cover to keep warm.

Discard all but 1 tablespoon of the fat from the skillet, add the shallots, and cook over medium heat, stirring, for 1 minute. Add the wine and reduce the liquid by half. Add the stock and simmer until reduced to 1½ cups. Bring the liquid to a boil, stir in the arrowroot mixture, then whisk it into the pot and continue to whisk until the sauce thickens slightly. Swirl in the butter, a little at a time. Strain the sauce into a bowl and divide it between the four serving plates. Top each serving of sauce with a veal chop and sprinkle with the chives. **Serves 4.**

Carré d'Agneau au Sauce Poivrade

Roast Rack of Lamb with Peppercorn Sauce

Here is the perfect entrée for an intimate dinner party ~
French cuisine having taught the world that there are few
more elegant ways of serving lamb than on the rack.
Anticipate that each rack will probably contain seven or eight
rib chops in all, and ask the butcher to trim them for you.
The best way to crush the peppercorns is to wrap them first in
plastic wrap or a towel, and then
to smash them with a mallet.

2 (1¼-pound) racks of lamb,
   trimmed
2 tablespoons olive oil
2 teaspoons dried rosemary,
   crumbled
Salt & pepper
2 tablespoons butter
⅓ cup minced shallots

2 teaspoons coarsely crushed black
   peppercorns
½ cup dry white wine
2 cups Beef Stock (p. 11)
   or canned broth
2 teaspoons tomato paste
1 tablespoon arrowroot dissolved in
   2 tablespoons dry white wine

Rub both racks of lamb with the olive oil, rosemary, and salt and pepper, and let them stand at room temperature for 30 minutes to 1 hour.

Preheat the oven to 500°F. Arrange the racks of lamb, fat-side up, in a large oven-proof skillet and roast for 10 minutes. Reduce the oven temperature to 400°F. and continue to roast the lamb for 10 to 12 minutes longer for medium-rare meat.

Transfer the racks to a serving platter, cover loosely with foil, and let stand for 10 minutes.

Meanwhile, discard the fat in the skillet. Add the butter and shallots and cook over medium-high heat, stirring, for 1 minute. Add the crushed peppercorns and wine and reduce the liquid by half. Add the stock and tomato paste, bring the liq-uid to a boil, and reduce by half. Stir the arrowroot mixture, then add it, in a stream, to the boiling reduced sauce and whisk over medium heat until thickened.

Carve the racks into chops, divide the sauce onto four serving plates, and arrange the lamb chops over each serving of sauce. **Serves 4.**

Navarin d'Agneau Printanière

Lamb Stew with Spring Vegetables

The French have wonderful ways of preparing lamb, among them this stew *à la printanière,* meaning with spring vegetables. Do not let the season prevent you from making this masterpiece year-round, though ~ it was given its name before improved transportation allowed vegetables that were out of season in one part of the country to be brought in from another.

3 tablespoons vegetable oil

2 pounds boneless lamb shoulder,
    cut into 2-inch pieces &
    patted dry

Salt & pepper

1 onion, coarsely chopped

1 carrot, sliced

3 tablespoons flour

4 cups Beef Stock (p. 11)
    or canned broth

1 cup drained & chopped canned
    tomatoes

½ cup dry white wine

2 garlic cloves, minced

1 teaspoon dried rosemary, crumbled

1 teaspoon dried thyme, crumbled

1 bay leaf

½ pound small white onions

½ pound baby carrots, peeled &
    trimmed

½ pound very small new potatoes,
    scrubbed

1 cup peas

In a casserole over medium-high heat, warm the vegetable oil until hot. Add the lamb and salt and pepper and brown it on all sides. Transfer the lamb to a platter.

Add the chopped onion and carrot to the casserole and cook over medium heat, stir-

ring occasionally, for 3 minutes. Add the flour and cook, stirring, for 2 minutes. Add the stock, tomatoes, wine, garlic, rosemary, thyme, and bay leaf, and bring to a boil.

Return the lamb to the casserole, cover, and simmer for 1 to 1½ hours, or until it is tender.

Using a fork, remove the lamb pieces to another casserole. Skim the fat from the surface of the cooking liquid and reduce the liquid over high heat until slightly thickened. Strain the thickened liquid over the lamb. Bring the mixture to a boil and add the onions. Simmer, covered, for 5 minutes. Add the carrots and potatoes, and simmer for 5 minutes. Add the peas and simmer for 5 minutes longer, or until the vegetables are tender. **Serves 4 to 6.**

Haricots Verts à l'Anglaise

Buttered Green Beans

True French *haricots verts* are deemed the best green beans grown. They are slim and tender (yet still crunchy) and require nothing more than the simple preparation that is given below. Though rather costly and not always easy to find, they are worth the search and the expense. If you substitute regular green beans, just make sure they are not too big or woody in texture. If desired, sprinkle the finished dish with grated lemon zest.

1 pound haricots verts or tender young green beans

2 tablespoons butter, softened
Salt & pepper

Bring a saucepan of salted water to a boil over medium-high heat. Add the beans and cook for 6 to 7 minutes, or until tender. Drain the beans, toss them with the butter, and season with salt and pepper. **Serves** 4.

Petits Pois à la Française

Peas Braised with Lettuce and Pearl Onions

A la française clearly says it all ~ in the French style. Long considered to be the finest way of preparing sweet young peas, the method has yet to be improved upon. Freshly shelled peas are best; if unavailable, frozen *petits pois* can be used.

¼ cup butter

*1 cup pearl onions, trimmed &
    peeled*

*1 large head lettuce, such as Boston,
    rinsed, dried, & cut into
    julienne strips*

3 pounds fresh peas, shelled

1 teaspoon dried thyme

1 bay leaf

Salt & pepper

½ teaspoon sugar

½ cup water

*¼ cup minced fresh mint leaves
    (optional)*

In a saucepan over medium heat, melt the butter. Add the onions and cook, stirring occasionally, for 5 minutes. Add the lettuce, peas, thyme, bay leaf, and salt and pepper, and cook, stirring occasionally, for 3 minutes. Add the sugar and water and simmer, covered, for 20 minutes, or until the peas are just tender. Remove and discard the bay leaf. Stir in the mint, if desired. **Serves 4.**

Artichauts à la Barigoule

Braised Artichokes with Mushrooms and Onions

These artichokes acquire a lovely, aromatic flavor from the vegetables and *bouquet garni* with which they are braised. Choose artichokes with smooth skins and tightly closed leaves; be sure to wash them well by immersing and shaking in a large pan of water, tip-side down ~ as dirt may be lodged in between the leaves.

4 medium artichokes

1 lemon, halved

Salt & pepper

¼ cup olive oil

2 cups small white onions, peeled

2 carrots, sliced

¼ pound mushrooms, sliced

2 garlic cloves, minced

⅓ cup white wine vinegar

½ cup dry white wine

1½ cups Chicken Stock (p. 10)
  or canned broth

Bouquet garni of 1 (4-inch) stalk
  celery, the white part of
  1 small leek, 1 sprig of thyme,
  & 1 bay leaf (tied together
  with string)

Cut off the top third of each artichoke, rub the cut edges with a lemon half, and trim the stem. With scissors, snip off the small leaves at the base and the points of the leaves. Scoop out the choke of each artichoke with a spoon and season the inside with lemon juice and salt and pep-per. Rub all cut surfaces with a lemon half and transfer the artichokes to a bowl of cold water. Squeeze the juice of the lemon into the bowl.

In a saucepan over medium heat, warm the oil until hot. Add the onions and car-rots and cook the vegetables, stirring

occasionally, for 5 minutes. Add the mushrooms, garlic, and salt and pepper, and cook the mixture, stirring, for 3 minutes. Add the artichokes, turn them to coat with the oil, then add the vinegar, wine, stock, and *bouquet garni*. Bring the liquid to a boil, then cover the mixture with a buttered round of wax paper and the lid, and braise, basting the artichokes with the cooking liquid once or twice, for 30 to 40 minutes, or until the artichokes are tender. Serve the vegetables with a little sauce poured over the top. **Serves** 4.

Endives Braisées

Braised Belgian Endive

We know and welcome the slightly bitter flavor of Belgian endive when it is used raw in salads. When endive is braised in butter, though, something interesting happens: It mellows somewhat in flavor and turns softer in texture. This vegetable side dish is particularly well suited to veal.

4 heads Belgian endive, trimmed
& washed
2 tablespoons butter
2 teaspoons lemon juice, or to taste

1 teaspoon sugar
Salt & pepper
1 tablespoon minced fresh parsley

Preheat the oven to 350°F. Butter a deep ovenproof skillet with a lid (or a small casserole), and arrange the endive in one layer. Dot with butter and sprinkle with lemon juice, sugar, and salt and pepper. Add enough water to measure ½ inch in the pan and cover the surface with a buttered round of wax paper. Cover the skillet or casserole with the lid. Braise the endive in the oven for 30 to 40 minutes, or until tender, turning occasionally and adding more water if necessary to prevent the endive from burning. Sprinkle with parsley. **Serves** 4.

Champignons et Oignons à la Grêcque

Marinated Mushrooms and Onions

For added variety, this dish can be made with any number of
vegetables, including cauliflower, fennel, and leeks.

⅓ cup olive oil

*1 pound small white onions,
    trimmed & peeled*

*2 pounds button mushrooms, stems
    trimmed & wiped clean with
    dampened paper towels*

*1 (16-ounce) can whole peeled toma-
    toes, puréed with their liquid*

*1 cup Chicken Stock (p. 10)
    or canned broth*

½ cup dry white wine

¼ cup lemon juice, or to taste

*Bouquet garni of 12 parsley stems,
    2 bay leaves, 2 tablespoons
    coriander seeds, 1 tablespoon
    peppercorns, & 2 teaspoons
    dried thyme (in a cheese-
    cloth bag)*

Salt

In a large saucepan or deep skillet over medium heat, warm the oil until hot. Add the onions and cook, stirring occasionally, for about 5 minutes, or until golden brown. Add the mushrooms and cook the mixture, stirring occasionally, for 5 minutes. Add the puréed tomatoes, stock, wine, lemon juice, *bouquet garni,* and salt, and bring to a boil. Boil the mixture, shaking the pan occasionally, for 15 to 20 minutes, or until the liquid is slightly thickened and the vegetables are tender. Remove the *bouquet garni*, pour the mixture into a bowl, and let it cool. Serve the vegetables at room temperature or chilled. **Serves 4 to 6.**

Légumes Grillés

Assorted Grilled Vegetables

Grilling has long been appreciated for the singular flavor it lends to meat and poultry, and should be equally celebrated for its effect on vegetables. This lovely assortment can be embellished with tender young zucchini, whole scallions, and even baby eggplants. Drizzle vinaigrette over the warm vegetables, if desired.

2 tomatoes, halved & cored

2 summer squash, halved lengthwise

1 red bell pepper, cored, seeded, & quartered

1 green bell pepper, cored, seeded, & quartered

1 yellow bell pepper, cored, seeded, & quartered

2 heads Belgian endive, trimmed & halved lengthwise

Extra-virgin olive oil

Salt & pepper

Preheat the grill according to the manufacturer's directions and arrange a grill rack about 5 inches from the coals. Brush the vegetables with the olive oil and season with salt and pepper. Arrange the vegetables in a grill basket and grill them, turning the basket once, for 6 to 8 minutes, or until tender. **Serves 4.**

Ratatouille

Eggplant and Zucchini with Tomatoes

The hot sun and long growing days of Provence conspire
to produce the wonderful ingredients that figure in
this extraordinary vegetable stew. Use it as a salad, as a side
dish, as a filling for *crêpes* and sandwiches, or as a
topping for *canapés*.

1 (1½- to 2-pound) eggplant, peeled
& cut into 1-inch cubes

Salt

½ cup olive oil

2 zucchini, cut into ¼-inch slices

1 large red bell pepper, cored,
seeded, & sliced

1 large green bell pepper, cored,
seeded, & sliced

1 large onion, sliced

2 cups peeled, seeded, & chopped
tomatoes

1 tablespoon tomato paste

1 tablespoon minced garlic

⅓ cup minced fresh basil leaves or
2 teaspoons dried

1 teaspoon dried thyme

1 bay leaf

Freshly ground black pepper

In a colander, toss the eggplant with salt and let its bitter juices drain off for 20 minutes. Pat dry. Preheat the oven to 350°F.

In a large skillet over medium heat, warm 2 tablespoons of the oil until hot. Add half the eggplant and cook, stirring occasionally, for 5 to 7 minutes, or until soft. With a slotted spoon, transfer the eggplant to a casserole. Repeat with the

remaining eggplant and 2 more tablespoons of the oil.

In the same skillet over medium heat, cook the zucchini in 1 tablespoon of the remaining oil, stirring occasionally, for 3 minutes. With a slotted spoon, transfer the zucchini to the casserole. Add the bell peppers and 2 tablespoons of the remaining oil to the skillet and cook, stirring occasionally, for 5 minutes, or until softened. With a slotted spoon, transfer the

bell peppers to the casserole.

Still using the same skillet, over medium-high heat, sauté the onion in the remaining 1 tablespoon oil, stirring occasionally, for 7 minutes, or until golden. Add the onion to the casserole, followed by the tomatoes, tomato paste, garlic, basil, thyme, bay leaf, and salt and pepper. Stir to combine, cover and bake the *ratatouille* in the middle of the oven for 30 minutes. **Serves 4 to 6.**

Signs for vins de pays, Languedoc

Pommes Frites

Crisp on the outside, meltingly soft within, *pommes frites* are
the perfect accompaniment to steak of any kind or sautéed
fish. One of the keys to making them as well as the French do
is to heat the deep-frying oil to the proper temperature and to
add the potatoes in batches ~ not
allowing the temperature of the oil to decrease significantly
when the potatoes are added. When one batch is done, remove
it for draining, then be sure to let the oil return to
the proper temperature before adding the next.

2 pounds baking potatoes

Oil for deep-frying

Salt

Peel the potatoes and cut them into ¼-inch sticks, dropping them into a bowl of cold water as they are cut. Drain the potatoes and pat them completely dry.

In a deep-fryer, heat 3 inches of oil to 380°F. on a deep-fat thermometer. Fry the potatoes in two to three batches, turning them, for 6 to 7 minutes, or until golden. With a slotted spoon, transfer the potatoes to a shallow pan lined with paper towels to drain. Sprinkle with salt. **Serves 6.**

Pommes Anna

Potato Cake

This "cake" depends on just butter and potatoes for its amazing flavor and texture. Although the directions are not complex, arranging the bottom layer of potatoes in an attractive pattern can take some practice. Note that the bottom layer becomes the top layer after the cake is unmolded. This vegetable side dish makes a splendid accompaniment to roasted or grilled meats.

6 tablespoons butter, melted
2 pounds boiling potatoes, peeled &
cut into ⅛-inch-thick slices
Salt & pepper

Preheat the oven to 450°F. Grease the bottom of a 9-inch nonstick cake pan or ovenproof skillet with 2 tablespoons of the butter. Arrange a layer of potatoes in concentric circles on the bottom of the pan, overlapping the slices slightly. Drizzle the potatoes with 1 tablespoon of the butter and sprinkle with salt and pepper. Continue to layer the remaining potatoes in circles until they reach the top edge of the pan, drizzling each layer with butter and seasoning with salt and pepper. Cover the top with a buttered round of foil. Weight the potatoes with a heavy saucepan placed directly on the foil. Cook the potatoes over medium heat for 5 minutes.

With the weight still in place, transfer the potatoes to the oven and bake for 30 minutes. Remove the weight and foil and bake the potatoes for 20 to 30 minutes

longer, or until the potatoes are tender and the top is golden. Invert a serving dish over the skillet and, holding the skillet and the dish together, invert the potato cake. Carefully unmold the potato cake onto the dish. **Serves 6.**

An open-air market in Gascony

Salade Verte avec Sauce Vinaigrette

Green Salad with Oil and Vinegar Dressing

In France, the salad is traditionally served after the main course, before the cheese and dessert courses. It is most interesting when prepared with a variety of greens. You might consider radicchio or sprigs of watercress for a somewhat peppery taste. Remember to wash and dry the leaves well. As to the dressing, it should only coat the leaves lightly ~ for an overdressed salad soon turns soggy.

¾ pound tender lettuce greens, such as Bibb, mâche (lamb's lettuce), red leaf lettuce, or a combination of them

THE VINAIGRETTE:
2 tablespoons white wine or tarragon vinegar
2 teaspoons Dijon mustard
Salt & pepper
⅓-½ cup olive oil

Rinse and spin dry the lettuce greens.

To make the *vinaigrette*, in a small bowl, whisk the vinegar and mustard with the salt and pepper. Add the oil slowly, whisking until emulsified.

In a bowl, toss the greens with the *vinaigrette*. **Serves 6 (Makes ½ cup vinaigrette).**

Olive oil and olives from Provence

Vinaigrettes

The basic combination of oil and vinegar, also known as French dressing, depends upon a delicate balance between its two principal components. The usual ratio is three parts oil to one part vinegar, but this can, and should, be adjusted to taste. To assure complete emulsification when making a *vinaigrette*, always whisk the oil into the vinegar, not the other way around. The variations on *vinaigrette* are many, including the ones that follow. All of these recipes start with the basic *vinaigrette* for which instructions are provided on page 71.

Vinaigrette aux Herbes

Into 1 recipe *Vinaigrette*, stir 2 tablespoons minced fresh tarragon, chervil, basil, dill, or chives. **Makes ½ cup.**

Vinaigrette à la Moutarde

Using 1 recipe *Vinaigrette,* substitute 1 to 2 tablespoons coarse-grained mustard for the Dijon mustard. Stir in 2 tablespoons chopped fresh chives or scallion greens. **Makes ½ cup.**

Vinaigrette à la Crème

Into 1 recipe *Vinaigrette aux Herbes,* stir ¼ cup *crème fraîche* or sour cream. Serve on cold cooked chicken, vegetables, or fish. **Makes ¾ cup.**

Sauce Ravigote

Into 1 recipe *Vinaigrette aux Herbes,* stir 1 teaspoon each drained chopped capers and shallots. Serve on hot or cold beef, chicken, or fish. **Makes ½ cup.**

Mesclun avec Timbales de Chèvre

Mixed Baby Greens with Goat Cheese Timbales

The timbales that grace these salads of delicate greens are
nothing more than simple custards, made of only goat
cheese and egg. The salads reflect the earliest cuttings of a
summer garden. As a variation, serve the salads with
apple or pear slices.

*1 pound goat cheese, such as
Montrachet or Bucheron,
crumbled*

4 eggs

*¾ pound mesclun (mixed baby greens)
1 recipe Vinaigrette aux Herbes (p. 73)
Fresh thyme leaves and black olives
for garnish*

Preheat the oven to 350°F. In a food processor, combine the goat cheese and the eggs and process until smooth. Divide the cheese mixture among six well-buttered ½-cup ramekins and smooth the tops. Set the ramekins in a shallow baking pan and add enough hot water to come halfway up the sides. Bake for 20 to 25 minutes, or until the tops are puffed and golden. Remove the timbales from the water bath and let cool until warm.

In a large bowl, toss the mesclun with the vinaigrette. Invert one timbale onto each of six serving plates and surround each one with salad. Garnish each timbale with thyme leaves and olives. **Serves 6.**

Pain Français

F r e n c h   B r e a d

En touts parts, all over France, you will see men, women, and children carrying bread home from their neighborhood *boulangeries.* It is a cultural and culinary given in France, as necessary a part of the meal as the wine the French drink and the air they breathe.

While everyone acknowledges that it is easier to buy French bread than it is to bake it, the pleasures derived from making your own will far outweigh any reservations you may initially have about undertaking the task. The recipe is long, but it is not complicated. From start to finish it will take about five hours; don't be impatient and do not rush the rising times. To achieve a light yet substantial crumb and a crisp, chewy crust, we recommend using bread flour and unglazed terra-cotta tiles for your oven. French bread is best eaten the day it is baked. However, it may be stored in the refrigerator, wrapped in plastic wrap, for one to two days. Crisp in the oven before serving.

1 package active dry yeast

A pinch of sugar

¼ cup warm water (108°-110°F.)

1 pound (about 3 cups) bread flour
   or unbleached flour

2 teaspoons salt

¾ cup water

Cornmeal

In a small bowl, proof the yeast with the sugar in the ¼ cup warm water for 5 minutes, or until the mixture is bubbling.

In a bowl, combine the flour and salt. Make a well in the center of the flour, add the yeast mixture and the ¾ cup water, and stir until the mixture forms a dough, adding more flour if the dough is too wet, and more water if the dough is too dry, 1 to 2 tablespoons at a time. (This will depend to a large extent upon the flour used and the humidity.) Turn the dough out onto a lightly floured surface and knead it for 2 to 3 minutes, or until it takes shape. Let the dough rest for 3 minutes. On a lightly floured surface, knead the dough for 6 to 8 minutes, or until it is smooth and elastic, adding more flour, a little at a time, if it begins to stick.

The dough may also be prepared in the food processor. In the food processor, combine the flour and salt and process the mixture for 5 seconds to blend. With the motor running, add the proofed yeast mixture and the ¾ cup water, and process until the dough just begins to form a ball, about 30 seconds, adding more water if the dough is too dry and more flour if the dough is too wet, 1 to 2 tablespoons at a time. Let the dough rest for 3 minutes. Knead the dough in the machine for 30 seconds more. Turn the dough out onto a lightly floured surface and knead it by hand for 2 to 3 minutes, or until it is smooth and elastic.

Transfer the dough to a bowl, cover it with plastic wrap, and let it rise in a warm, draft-free place for 1 hour, or until it is 1½ times its original size. Punch down the dough and pat it into a ¼-inch-thick rectangle. Fold one long side of the dough to meet the middle and fold the other side over it. Again, flatten the dough into a rectangle and fold it lengthwise in three as described above. Fold the dough over and transfer it to the bowl, smooth-side up. Cover it with plastic wrap, and let it rise for 1 to 1½ hours, or until it is 2½ to 3 times its size.

Punch down the dough and divide it in half. Cover one-half with plastic wrap or an inverted bowl while working with the other half. On a lightly floured work surface, pat the dough into a rectangle about 14 inches long, fold it in half lengthwise, then firmly press and flatten the entire dough surface, especially the seam. Rotate the dough so that the seam is on top. With your fingertips, gently press the dough along the seam to create a crease. Fold the dough in half lengthwise along the crease. Firmly press and flatten the entire dough surface, but especially the seam.

Form the dough into a long loaf by rolling it back and forth under your hands, beginning at the center of the loaf and working out towards the ends, forming the ends into smooth points. Roll the dough in this manner until it extends 12 to 14 inches in length. Pinch the seam together to seal, then transfer the dough, seam-side down, to a lightly floured towel to rise. Dust the dough with flour, then loosely cover it with another towel.

Form the remaining dough in the same manner. Let the loaves rise for 1 to 1½ hours, or until doubled in bulk.

To simulate a baker's oven, arrange unglazed terra-cotta tiles or a pizza stone on the lowest rack of your oven. Put a heavy ovenproof skillet or baking pan on the floor of the oven and preheat the oven to 450°F. Sprinkle a baker's peel, pizza board, or flat baking sheet with cornmeal and roll the loaves onto it. With a single-edged razor, cut 3 diagonal slits, about ½ inch deep, in

A wood-fired bread oven, near Perigueux

the top of each loaf. Slide the loaves onto the tiles and quickly pour about 1 cup water into the pan on the bottom of the oven. Immediately close the oven door before the steam escapes. The steam will help the bread form a crusty coating. Bake for 20 minutes. If the loaves brown too quickly, cover with a sheet of foil. Lower the oven temperature to 400°F. and bake for 10 minutes more, or until the loaves sound hollow when tapped. Turn off the oven. Let the loaves stand in the oven for 5 minutes more. Transfer the loaves to a rack and let cool completely. **Makes 2 loaves.**

Poires au Vin Rouge

Pears Poached in Red Wine

Poached pears appear frequently on the dessert tables of France. Some are poached in a simple sugar syrup, others in a flavored sugar syrup, and still others, like the ones below, are poached in sweetened red (or white) wine. These pears, which turn a magnificent rosy pink as they poach, are particularly pretty garnished with fresh mint.

4 firm ripe pears, such as Anjou, Bosc, or Bartlett

½ lemon

3 cups dry red wine

½ cup sugar

1 (2-inch) strip lemon peel

1 stick cinnamon, cracked

4 whole black peppercorns

4 whole cloves

1 vanilla bean, split lengthwise

Peel the pears and core them from the base, leaving the stems intact. Rub the pears with the lemon to prevent discoloration.

In a saucepan, combine the remaining ingredients and bring the liquid to a boil. Simmer the syrup, stirring occasionally, for 5 minutes, or until transparent. Add the pears, cover with wax paper, and cook at a bare simmer, turning the pears from time to time, for 20 to 25 minutes, or until just tender. Let the pears cool in the liquid.

With a slotted spoon, transfer the pears to a serving dish. Strain the cooking liquid into another saucepan and reduce it to 1 cup over medium-high heat. Let the syrup cool to warm and pour it over the pears. Cool to room temperature. Serve at room temperature or chilled. **Serves 4.**

Clafouti aux Cerises

Cherry Flan

Sometimes called a flan, sometimes called a pancake, and
sometimes even called a pudding, this famous dessert
comes from Limousin in the central southwest of France. It is
quite simple to prepare and fascinating to watch: It
puffs up uneven and craggy in the oven, then, once you
remove it, plummets back down in the baking pan.
This dessert can be made with a wide assortment of fruit,
including figs, apples, pears, and plums.

1 cup milk

½ cup heavy cream

⅓ cup sugar, or to taste

⅔ cup flour

2 eggs

1 egg yolk

1½ teaspoons vanilla extract

3 cups pitted Bing cherries or
    canned cherries, drained

Confectioners' sugar for the top

Preheat the oven to 375°F. In a blender or food processor, combine the milk, heavy cream, sugar, flour, eggs, egg yolk, and vanilla, and blend until smooth. Arrange the cherries in a buttered 10-inch pie plate and pour the batter over them. Bake for 35 to 45 minutes, or until the flan is puffed and golden. Sift the confectioners' sugar over the top and serve warm. **Serves 4 to 6.**

Pots de Crème au Chocolat

Individual Chocolate Custards

French *pots de crème* are egg-based custards that bake in the oven. They differ from English pudding, which is starch-based and cooks on the stove. For the most authentic rendition, serve the custards in the small covered *pots* for which the dessert was named. Chocolate curls are made by running a vegetable peeler along the side of a chocolate bar.

2 cups heavy cream

6 ounces dark sweet chocolate, cut into bits

⅓ cup sugar

4 egg yolks

1 teaspoon vanilla extract

Chocolate curls for garnish

Preheat the oven to 350°F. In a heavy saucepan, combine the cream and chocolate and cook over medium heat, stirring, until the chocolate is melted and the mixture is smooth. Whisk in the sugar, the yolks, one at a time, and the vanilla. Strain the custard into six ½-cup *pots de crème*, ramekins, or ovenproof ceramic cups, and place in a baking pan. Add enough hot water to the pan to reach halfway up the sides of the dishes. Bake for 25 minutes, or until the top is just set. Remove the ramekins from the pan and let cool. Garnish with the chocolate curls. **Serves 6.**

Crème Brûlée

Vanilla Custard with Caramel Topping

This exquisite, silky custard of eggs and heavy cream is
rendered even more appealing when it is topped with sugar
and passed under the broiler to form a caramelized crust. One
word of caution: Watch the custard carefully while the sugar
is caramelizing as it can burn easily.

6 egg yolks

⅓ cup plus 3 tablespoons sugar

3 cups heavy cream

1½ teaspoons vanilla extract

Preheat the oven to 325°F. In a bowl, whisk together the egg yolks and the ⅓ cup of sugar. In a saucepan, scald the cream over medium heat. In a stream, add the scalded cream to the egg yolks, stirring constantly. Stir in the vanilla. Strain the custard into six ⅓-cup ramekins and arrange the ramekins in a baking pan. Add enough hot water to the pan to reach halfway up the sides of the ramekins.

Cover the baking pan with aluminum foil and bake for 1¼ to 1½ hours, or until the custard is set around the edges but still slightly soft in the center. Let the custards cool, then chill them for at least 2 hours or overnight.

Preheat the broiler. Sprinkle the top of each chilled custard with some of the remaining sugar, spreading it in an even layer and being sure that the custard is

completely covered. Arrange the ramekins on a baking sheet and carefully place them under the broiler, about 5 inches from the heat. Broil the custards, turning the ramekins several times, until the tops are golden brown, about 5 minutes. Watch closely. Chill the custards for 2 hours before serving. **Serves 6.**

Tarte aux Poires

Pear Frangipane Tart

The *frangipane* (almond pastry cream) filling in this tart was named after the Marquis Muzio Frangipani, a sixteenth-century Italian nobleman who lived in Paris and concocted an almond-based perfume for scenting gloves. The filling puffs up beautifully when baked.

1 recipe Pâte Brisée (p. 13)

6 tablespoons butter, softened

⅓ cup sugar

2 eggs

1 cup blanched almonds, ground

1 teaspoon vanilla extract

3 poached pears, halved, cored, & thinly sliced (see photograph)

½ cup apricot preserves, strained

1 tablespoon Amaretto, cognac, or dark rum (optional)

Preheat the oven to 350°F. Line a 10-inch tart pan with the pastry and trim the edges. Chill for 30 minutes.

Using an electric mixer, cream the butter. Add the sugar and beat until fluffy. Add the eggs, one at a time, then beat in the almonds and vanilla. Spread the *frangipane* filling over the bottom of the shell. Using a spatula, transfer the pears to the top of the filling, placing them in a spoked pattern, narrow points facing center. Place the tart on a baking sheet and bake in the lower third of the oven for 45 minutes, or until the filling is golden and set. Let the tart cool on a rack. In a saucepan, combine the preserves and liqueur, if using, and bring to a simmer. Simmer for 2 minutes, stirring continuously. Spoon or brush the glaze on the cooled tart. **Serves 6 to 8.**

Sorbets aux Fruits

Assorted Fruit Sorbets

Sorbet is French fruit ice, made from only two components ~ a simple sugar syrup and either puréed fruit or fruit juice. If desired, a little fresh lemon juice can be added also, but that is all. Little wonder it is as refreshing as it is ~ there is nothing to complicate its pure flavor. The assortment of flavors below suggests only a few of the fruits that lend themselves to sorbet. Consider, too, lemon or orange or more exotic flavors like mango and passion fruit.

Pink Grapefruit Sorbet

1 cup sugar

1 cup water

2 cups strained pink grapefruit juice

In a saucepan over medium heat, combine the sugar and water. Bring the liquid to a simmer and cook, stirring, until the sugar is dissolved. Let cool, then cover and chill for 30 minutes.

In a large bowl, combine the chilled sugar syrup and the grapefruit juice and transfer the mixture to an ice-cream machine. Freeze according to the manufacturer's directions. **Makes about 1 quart.**

Raspberry Sorbet

1½ cups sugar

1½ cups water

1 pound fresh or frozen
    raspberries

2 tablespoons lemon
    juice, or to taste

Following the directions for Pink Grapefruit Sorbet, make the sugar syrup with 1½ cups each sugar and water. Chill as described.

In a food processor, purée the raspberries until smooth. Strain the purée through a sieve into a bowl and stir in the lemon juice. Add the sugar syrup to the purée and transfer it to an ice-cream machine. Freeze according to the manufacturer's directions. **Makes about 1 quart.**

Peach Sorbet

1 cup sugar

1 cup water

3 cups peeled diced peaches

2 to 3 tablespoons lemon
    juice, or to taste

Following the directions for Pink Grapefruit Sorbet, make the sugar syrup with the 1 cup each sugar and water. Chill as described.

In a food processor, purée the peaches until smooth. Transfer the purée to a large bowl and stir in the chilled sugar syrup and the lemon juice. Transfer the mixture to an ice-cream machine. Freeze according to the manufacturer's directions. **Makes about 1 quart.**

Soufflé au Chocolat

Chocolate Soufflé

The *soufflé* is the drama of French cooking at its highest, a dazzling way to end a well-cooked meal. This delectable chocolate *soufflé* is especially decadent when served with whipped cream, *crème anglaise,* or even warm chocolate sauce.

½ cup granulated sugar

¼ cup flour

1 cup milk

1 tablespoon butter

4 egg yolks

1 tablespoon vanilla

6 ounces dark sweet
   chocolate, melted

6 egg whites

Confectioners' sugar for the top

Preheat the oven to 400°F. Butter a 2-quart *soufflé* dish. Sprinkle the *soufflé* dish with granulated sugar, shaking out the excess, then fit it with a buttered and sugared paper or foil collar that extends 2 inches above the rim of the dish.

In a bowl, whisk together ¼ cup of the granulated sugar, the flour, and ⅓ cup of the milk. Scald the remaining milk in a saucepan and add it to the bowl in a stream, whisking, until the mixture is smooth. Transfer the mixture to a saucepan, bring it to a simmer, whisking, and cook, continuing to whisk, for 3 minutes. Remove the pan from the heat and beat in the butter. Beat in the egg yolks, one yolk at a time, then the vanilla and the melted chocolate.

The medieval town of Carcassonne, Languedoc

In a bowl with an electric mixer, beat the egg whites until they hold soft peaks. Add the remaining granulated sugar, a little at a time, and beat until the whites hold stiff peaks. Stir one-fourth of the whites into the chocolate mixture, then fold in the remaining whites gently but thoroughly. Spoon the mixture into the prepared soufflé dish.

Place the *soufflé* in the oven and immediately reduce the oven temperature to 375°F. Bake the *soufflé* for 35 to 40 minutes, or until puffed. Sift the confectioners' sugar over the top and serve the *soufflé* at once. **Serves 6.**

WEIGHTS

OUNCES AND POUNDS	METRICS
¼ ounce	7 grams
⅓ ounce	10 grams
½ ounce	14 grams
1 ounce	28 grams
1¾ ounces	50 grams
2 ounces	57 grams
2⅔ ounces	75 grams
3 ounces	85 grams
3½ ounces	100 grams
4 ounces (¼ pound)	114 grams
6 ounces	170 grams
8 ounces (½ pound)	227 grams
9 ounces	250 grams
16 ounces (1 pound)	454 grams
1.1 pounds	500 grams
2.2 pounds	1,000 grams (1 kilogram)

TEMPERATURES

°F (FAHRENHEIT)	°C (CENTIGRADE OR CELSIUS)
32 (water freezes)	0
108-110 (warm)	42-43
140	60
203 (water simmers)	95
212 (water boils)	100
225 (very slow oven)	107.2
245	120
266	130
300 (slow oven)	149
350 (moderate oven)	177
375	191
400 (hot oven)	205
450	232
500 (very hot oven)	260

LIQUID MEASURES

tsp.: teaspoon
Tbs.: tablespoon

SPOONS AND CUPS	METRIC EQUIVALENTS
1 tsp.	5 milliliters (5 grams)
2 tsp.	10 milliliters (10 grams)
3 tsp. (1 Tbs.)	15 milliliters (15 grams)
3⅓ Tbs.	½ deciliter (50 milliliters)
¼ cup	59 milliliters
⅓ cup	1 deciliter less 1⅓ Tbs.

SPOONS AND CUPS	METRIC EQUIVALENTS
⅓ cup + 1 Tbs.	1 deciliter (100 milliliters)
1 cup	¼ liter less 1¼ Tbs.
1 cup + 1¼ Tbs.	¼ liter
2 cups	½ liter less 2½ Tbs.
2 cups + 2½ Tbs.	½ liter
4 cups	1 liter less 1 deciliter
4⅓ cups	1 liter (1,000 milliliters)

INDEX

Picture Credits

Boys Syndication/Michael Boys: 1; 2-3; 37; 66; 69; 70; 72; 88; 93; 96.

Jean Buldain/Picture Perfect: 15. Elizabeth Watt: 17; 31; 43.

Richard Felber: 33. Steve Needham: 18; 28. Anthony Blake/Picture

Perfect: 21; 45; 51; 59; 87. Martin Jacobs: 22; 55; 81.

Charlie Waite/Picture Perfect: 24. Mick Rock/Picture Perfect; 79.

Alan Richardson: 35; 38; 47; 63; 75. Food and Wines from France: 41.

Marie Claire/Ryman-Cabannes 49.

Marie Claire/Bouchet, Le Foll: 83. Ellen Silverman: 53; 84.